D0376082

To:

_____

From:

_____

Date:

_____

© 2010 Summerside Press™
Minneapolis 55438
www.summersidepress.com

God Comforts You

A *Pocket Inspirations* Book

ISBN 978-1-60936-021-4

Scripture references are from the following sources: The Holy Bible, King James Version (KJV). The Holy Bible, New International Version®, NIV®. Copyright © 1973, 1978, 1984 by Biblica, Inc.™ Used by permission of Zondervan. All rights reserved worldwide. The New King James Version (NKJV). Copyright © 1982 by Thomas Nelson, Inc. Used by permission. The New American Standard Bible® (NASB), Copyright © 1960, 1962, 1963, 1968, 1971, 1972, 1973, 1975, 1977, 1995 by The Lockman Foundation. Used by permission. The Holy Bible, New Living Translation (NLT), copyright 1996, 2004. Used by permission of Tyndale House Publishers, Inc., Wheaton, Illinois. The Message (MSG). Copyright © 1993, 1994, 1995, 1996, 2000, 2001, 2002 by Eugene Peterson. Used by permission of NavPress, Colorado Springs, CO. The Living Bible (TLB) © 1971. Used by permission of Tyndale House Publishers, Inc., Wheaton, Illinois 60189. All rights reserved.

Excluding Scripture verses and deity pronouns, in some quotations references to men and masculine pronouns have been replaced with gender-neutral or feminine references. Additionally, in some quotations we have carefully updated verb forms and wordings that may distract modern readers.

Compiled by Marilyn Jansen and Barbara Farmer
Designed by Mick Thurber

Summerside Press™ is an inspirational publisher offering fresh, irresistible books to uplift the heart and engage the mind.

Printed in USA.

God Comforts You

PROMISES FOR LIFE

summerside
PRESS™

God's Compassion

Remember my affliction and my wandering....
Surely my soul remembers
And is bowed down within me.
This I recall to my mind,
Therefore I have hope.
The LORD's lovingkindnesses indeed never cease,
For His compassions never fail.
They are new every morning;
Great is Your faithfulness.
"The LORD is my portion," says my soul,
"Therefore I have hope in Him."
The LORD is good to those who wait for Him,
To the person who seeks Him.
It is good that he waits silently
For the salvation of the LORD.

LAMENTATIONS 3:19–26 NASB

The loving God we serve has immeasurable
compassion and tenderness toward each of us
throughout our lives.

DR. JAMES DOBSON

Compassion for others comes when
we see ourselves as God sees us.

JANETTE OKE

God is always speaking to us.
Listen to Him. He wants from us
deep love, compassion, and forgiveness.

MOTHER TERESA

The compassionate person feels with God's heart.

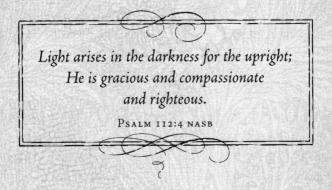

Light arises in the darkness for the upright;
He is gracious and compassionate
and righteous.

PSALM 112:4 NASB

The Weaver

My life is but a weaving
Between my Lord and me,
I cannot choose the colors
He worketh steadily.
Oftimes He weaveth sorrow,
And I in foolish pride
Forget He sees the upper
And I, the underside....
The dark threads are as needful
In the Weaver's skillful hand
As the threads of gold and silver
In the pattern He has planned.

There are those who suffer greatly, and yet,
through the recognition that pain can be
a thread in the pattern of God's weaving,
find the way to a fundamental joy.

For whatever life holds for you and your family in the coming days, weave the unfailing fabric of God's Word through your heart and mind. It will hold strong, even if the rest of life unravels.

GIGI GRAHAM TCHIVIDJIAN

There may be times in your life when it all seems dark and you cannot see or trace the hand of God, but yet God is working. Just as much as He works in the bright sunlight, He works all through the night.

Blessed are they that mourn: for they shall be comforted.

MATTHEW 5:4 KJV

Comforted by God

Blessed be the God and Father of our Lord
Jesus Christ, the Father of mercies and God
of all comfort, who comforts us in all our
affliction so that we will be able
to comfort those who are in any affliction
with the comfort with which we ourselves
are comforted by God.

2 CORINTHIANS 1:3–4 KJV

May our Lord Jesus Christ himself and God
our Father, who loved us and by his grace
gave us eternal comfort and a wonderful
hope, comfort you and strengthen you in
every good thing you do and say.

2 THESSALONIANS 2:16–17 NLT

All [God's] glory and beauty come from within, and there He delights to dwell. His visits there are frequent, His conversation sweet, His comforts refreshing, His peace passing all understanding.

THOMAS À KEMPIS

Only God can truly comfort; He comes alongside us and shows us how deeply and tenderly He feels for us in our sorrow.

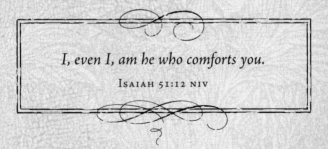

I, even I, am he who comforts you.

ISAIAH 51:12 NIV

Treasure in Nature

If we are children of God, we have a tremendous
treasure in nature and will realize that it is holy
and sacred. We will see God reaching out to us in
every wind that blows, every sunrise and sunset,
every cloud in the sky, every flower that blooms,
and every leaf that fades.

OSWALD CHAMBERS

Look up at all the stars in the night sky and hear
your Father saying, "I carefully set each one
in its place. Know that I love you more than these."
Sit by the lake's edge, listening to the water
lapping the shore and hear your Father gently
calling you to that place near His heart.

WENDY MOORE

What a wildly wonderful world, GOD!
You made it all, with Wisdom at your side,
made earth overflow with your wonderful creations.

PSALM 104:24 MSG

I love to think of nature as an unlimited
broadcasting station through which God speaks
to us every hour, if only we will tune in.

GEORGE WASHINGTON CARVER

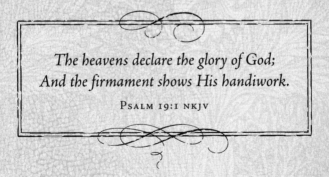

The heavens declare the glory of God;
And the firmament shows His handiwork.

PSALM 19:1 NKJV

The Grace of God

God, being rich in mercy, because of His great love
with which He loved us, even when we were dead
in our transgressions, made us alive together with
Christ (by grace you have been saved), and raised
us up with Him, and seated us with Him in the
heavenly places in Christ Jesus, so that in the ages
to come He might show the surpassing riches of
His grace in kindness toward us in Christ Jesus.
For by grace you have been saved through faith; and
that not of yourselves, it is the gift of God; not as
a result of works, so that no one may boast. For we
are His workmanship, created in Christ Jesus for
good works, which God prepared beforehand so
that we would walk in them.

EPHESIANS 2:4–10 NASB

Faith is a living, daring confidence in God's grace, so sure and certain that a man could stake his life on it a thousand times.

MARTIN LUTHER

Grace means that God already loves us as much as an infinite God can possibly love.

PHILIP YANCEY

God is able to make all grace abound to you, so that...having all that you need, you will abound in every good work.

2 CORINTHIANS 9:8 NIV

In the Silence

Our Father, sometimes You seem so far away, as if
You are a God in hiding, as if You are determined
to elude all who seek You.... At times when we feel
forsaken, may we know the presence of the Holy
Spirit who brings comfort to all human hearts
when we are willing to surrender ourselves.

PETER MARSHALL

Be it ours, when we cannot see the face of God,
to trust under the shadow of His wings.

CHARLES H. SPURGEON

God's peace...is far more wonderful than the human
mind can understand. His peace will keep your
thoughts and your hearts quiet and at rest.

PHILIPPIANS 4:7 TLB

The soul is a temple, and God is
silently building it by night and by day.
Precious thoughts are building it;
unselfish love is building it;
all-penetrating faith is building it.

HENRY WARD BEECHER

I believe in the sun even when it is not shining.
I believe in love even when I do not feel it.
I believe in God even when He is silent.

The eternal God is your refuge, and
underneath are the everlasting arms.

DEUTERONOMY 33:27 NIV

God's Guidance

To You, O Lord, I lift up my soul. O my God, in You I trust, do not let me be ashamed; do not let my enemies exult over me. Indeed, none of those who wait for You will be ashamed.... Make me know Your ways, O Lord; teach me Your paths. Lead me in Your truth and teach me, for You are the God of my salvation; for You I wait all the day. Remember, O Lord, Your compassion and Your lovingkindnesses, for they have been from of old.

PSALM 25:1–6 NASB

God, who has led you safely on so far, will lead you on to the end. Be altogether at rest in the loving holy confidence which you ought to have in His heavenly Providence.

FRANCIS DE SALES

Strength, rest, guidance, grace, help,
sympathy, love—all from God to us!
What a list of blessings!

EVELYN STENBOCK

The Lord is able to guide. The promises
cover every imaginable situation....
Take the hand He stretches out.

ELISABETH ELLIOT

You guide me with your counsel,
leading me to a glorious destiny.

PSALM 73:24 NLT

Renewed Strength

Why do you say...
"My way is hidden from the LORD..."?
Do you not know? Have you not heard?
The LORD is the everlasting God,
the Creator of the ends of the earth.
He will not grow tired or weary,
and his understanding no one can fathom....
Even youths grow tired and weary,
and young men stumble and fall;
but those who hope in the LORD
will renew their strength.
They will soar on wings like eagles;
they will run and not grow weary,
they will walk and not be faint.

ISAIAH 40:27–28, 30–31 NIV

Those who live prayerfully are constantly ready to receive the breath of God, and to let their lives be renewed and expanded.

HENRI J. M. NOUWEN

That is God's call to us—simply to be people who are content to live close to Him and to renew the kind of life in which the closeness is felt and experienced.

THOMAS MERTON

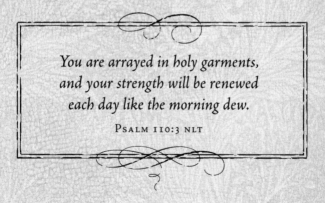

You are arrayed in holy garments, and your strength will be renewed each day like the morning dew.

PSALM 110:3 NLT

The Goodness of God

We walk without fear, full of hope and courage
and strength to do His will, waiting for the endless
good which He is always giving as fast
as He can get us able to take it in.

GEORGE MACDONALD

I would have despaired
unless I had believed that I would see
the goodness of the LORD
in the land of the living.
Wait for the LORD;
be strong and let your heart take courage;
yes, wait for the LORD.

PSALM 27:13–14 NASB

All that is good, all that is true, all that is beautiful,
all that is beneficent, be it great or small,
be it perfect or fragmentary, natural as well
as supernatural, moral as well as material,
comes from God.

JOHN HENRY NEWMAN

The goodness of God is infinitely more wonderful
than we will ever be able to comprehend.

A. W. TOZER

Open your eyes and see—how good God is.
Blessed are you who run to him.

PSALM 34:8–9 MSG

Place of Rest

Breathe, O breathe thy loving Spirit
into every troubled breast;
Let us all in thee inherit,
let us find thy promised rest.

CHARLES WESLEY

Trust Him when dark doubts assail thee
Trust Him when thy strength is small,
Trust Him when to simply trust Him
Seems the hardest thing of all.

Trust Him, He is ever faithful;
Trust Him, for His will is best;
Trust Him, for the Heart of Jesus,
Is the only place of rest.

In returning and rest you shall be saved;
In quietness and confidence shall be your strength.

ISAIAH 30:15 NKJV

In comparison with this big world, the human
heart is only a small thing. Though the world
is so large, it is utterly unable to satisfy this tiny
heart. Our ever growing soul and its capacities
can be satisfied only in the infinite God. As water
is restless until it reaches its level, so the soul
has no peace until it rests in God.

SADHU SUNDAR SINGH

Love comes while we rest against
our Father's chest. Joy comes when we
catch the rhythms of His heart. Peace comes
when we live in harmony with those rhythms.

KEN GIRE

Be still, and know that I am God!

PSALM 46:10 NLT

Mighty to Keep

God, who is our dwelling place, is also
our fortress. It can only mean one thing,
and that is, that if we will but live in
our dwelling place, we shall be perfectly
safe and secure from every assault.

HANNAH WHITALL SMITH

Whom have I in heaven but You?
And besides You, I desire nothing on earth.
My flesh and my heart may fail,
but God is the strength of my heart
and my portion forever....
As for me, the nearness of God is my good;
I have made the Lord GOD my refuge.

PSALM 73:25–26, 28 NASB

God promises to keep us in the palm
of [His] hand, with or without our awareness.
God has already made a space for us,
even if we have not made a space for God.

DAVID AND BARBARA SORENSEN

God is adequate as our keeper.... Your faith
will not fail while God sustains it;
you are not strong enough to fall away
while God is resolved to hold you.

J. I. PACKER

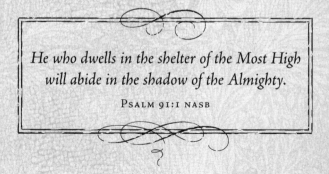

He who dwells in the shelter of the Most High
will abide in the shadow of the Almighty.

PSALM 91:1 NASB

A Life Transformed

To pray is to change. This is a great grace. How
good of God to provide a path whereby our
lives can be taken over by love and joy and peace
and patience and kindness and goodness and
faithfulness and gentleness and self-control.

RICHARD J. FOSTER

We, who with unveiled faces all reflect
the Lord's glory, are being transformed into
his likeness with ever-increasing glory,
which comes from the Lord, who is the Spirit.

2 CORINTHIANS 3:18 NIV

For God is, indeed, a wonderful Father
who longs to pour out His mercy upon us,
and whose majesty is so great that He can
transform us from deep within.

TERESA OF AVILA

Do not conform any longer to the pattern
of this world, but be transformed by
the renewing of your mind. Then you
will be able to test and approve what God's
will is—his good, pleasing and perfect will.

ROMANS 12:2 NIV

A life transformed by the power of God
is always a marvel and a miracle.

GERALDINE NICHOLAS

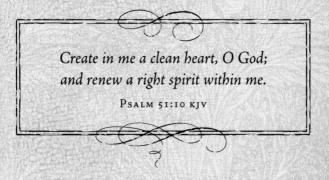

Create in me a clean heart, O God;
and renew a right spirit within me.

PSALM 51:10 KJV

Love Like That

Watch what God does, and then you do it,
like children who learn proper behavior from
their parents. Mostly what God does is love you.
Keep company with him and learn a life of love.
Observe how Christ loved us. His love was not
cautious but extravagant. He didn't love in order
to get something from us but to give everything
of himself to us. Love like that.

EPHESIANS 5:1–2 MSG

Let Jesus be in your heart,
Eternity in your spirit,
The world under your feet,
The will of God in your actions.
And let the love of God shine forth from you.

CATHERINE OF GENOA

Dear friends, since God so loved us, we also ought to love one another.... If we love one another, God lives in us and his love is made complete in us.

1 JOHN 4:11–12 NIV

Open your hearts to the love God instills.... God loves you tenderly. What He gives you is not to be kept under lock and key, but to be shared.

MOTHER TERESA

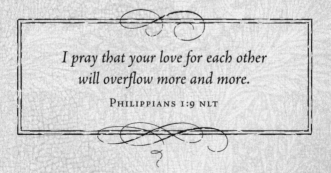

I pray that your love for each other will overflow more and more.

PHILIPPIANS 1:9 NLT

Overcoming

Christ desires to be with you in whatever crisis
you may find yourself. Call upon His name.
See if He will not do as He promised He would.
He will not make your problems go away, but He
will give you the power to deal with and overcome
them.... Suffering is endurable if we do not have
to bear it alone; and the more compassionate
the Presence, the less acute the pain.

BILLY GRAHAM

"They will fight against you but will
not overcome you, for I am with you
and will rescue you," declares the LORD.

JEREMIAH 1:19 NIV

God can take tragedy and turn it into triumph.
He routinely does this for those who love Him.

DR. JAMES DOBSON

The world is full of suffering.
It is also full of the overcoming of it.

<small>HELEN KELLER</small>

He did not say, "You will never have a rough
passage, you will never be over-strained,
you will never feel uncomfortable," but He did say,
"You will never be overcome."

<small>JULIAN OF NORWICH</small>

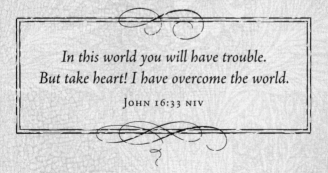

In this world you will have trouble.
But take heart! I have overcome the world.

<small>JOHN 16:33 NIV</small>

Free to Live

God, your God, will cut away the thick calluses
on your heart and your children's hearts,
freeing you to love God, your God, with your
whole heart and soul and live, really live....
And you will make a new start, listening
obediently to God, keeping all his
commandments that I'm commanding
you today. God, your God, will outdo
himself in making things go well for you....
Love God, your God. Walk in his ways.
Keep his commandments, regulations,
and rules so that you will live, really live,
live exuberantly, blessed by God....
Love God, your God, listening obediently
to him, firmly embracing him.
Oh yes, he is life itself.

Deuteronomy 30:6–9, 16, 20 msg

Praise is a place for God to be. A home place.
A workshop for His Holy Spirit in our lives.
It is an atmosphere of total openness where He can
be free to do good things in and through our days.

GLORIA GAITHER

I asked God for all things that I might enjoy life.
He gave me life that I might enjoy all things.

Let my soul be at rest again, for the LORD
has been good to me....
And so I walk in the LORD's presence
as I live here on earth!

PSALM 116:7, 9 NLT

Seek First

Look at the birds of the air, that they do not sow,
nor reap nor gather into barns, and yet
your heavenly Father feeds them.
Are you not worth much more than they?
And who of you by being worried
can add a single hour to his life?
And why are you worried about clothing?
Observe how the lilies of the field grow;
they do not toil nor do they spin,
yet I say to you that not even Solomon in all
his glory clothed himself like one of these.
But if God so clothes the grass of the field,
which is alive today and tomorrow
is thrown into the furnace,
will He not much more clothe you?
You of little faith! Do not worry then, saying,
"What will we eat?" or "What will we drink?"
or "What will we wear for clothing?"
For...your heavenly Father knows
that you need all these things....

But seek first His kingdom and His righteousness,
and all these things will be added to you.

MATTHEW 6:26–33 NASB

Trust the past to the mercy of God,
the present to His love,
and the future to His Providence.

AUGUSTINE

Ask and it will be given to you;
seek and you will find;
knock and door will be opened to you.

MATTHEW 7:7 NIV

By Love Alone

By love alone is God enjoyed; by love alone
delighted in, by love alone approached and admired.
His nature requires love.

Thomas Traherne

There is an essential connection between
experiencing God, loving God, and trusting God.
You will trust God only as much as you love Him,
and you will love Him to the extent you have
touched Him, rather that He has touched you.

Brennan Manning

Although it be good to think upon the kindness of
God, and to love Him and worship Him for it; yet
it is far better to gaze upon the pure essence of Him
and to love Him and worship Him for Himself.

We desire many things, and God offers us only one thing. He can offer us only one thing— Himself. He has nothing else to give. There is nothing else to give.

PETER KREEFT

The reason for loving God is God Himself, and the measure in which we should love Him is to love Him without measure.

BERNARD OF CLAIRVAUX

Love the LORD your God with all your heart, all your soul, and all your strength.

DEUTERONOMY 6:5 NLT

Restoration

The Spirit of the Sovereign LORD is on me,
because the LORD has anointed me
to preach good news to the poor.
He has sent me to bind up the brokenhearted,
to proclaim freedom for the captives and
release from darkness for the prisoners,
to proclaim the year of the LORD's favor
and the day of vengeance of our God,
to comfort all who mourn,
and provide for those who grieve in Zion—
to bestow on them a crown of beauty
instead of ashes, the oil of gladness
instead of mourning, and a garment of praise
instead of a spirit of despair.
They will be called oaks of righteousness,
a planting of the LORD
for the display of his splendor.

ISAIAH 61:1–3 NIV

The Lord promises to bind up the brokenhearted,
to give relief and full deliverance to those whose
spirits have been weighed down.

CHARLES R. SWINDOLL

I can drink freely of God's power and experience
His touch of refreshment and blessing—much like
an invigorating early spring rain.

ANABEL GILLHAM

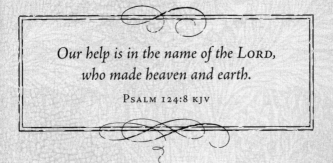

Our help is in the name of the LORD,
who made heaven and earth.

PSALM 124:8 KJV

Steps of Faith

In the dark dreary nights, when the storm is at
its most fierce, the lighthouse burns bright so the
sailors can find their way home again. In life the
same light burns. This light is fueled with love,
faith, and hope. And through life's most
fierce storms these three burn their brightest
so we also can find our way home again.

Why should we live halfway up the hill and
swathed in the mists, when we might have
an unclouded sky and a radiant sun over
our heads if we would climb higher
and walk in the light of His face?

ALEXANDER MACLAREN

Faith goes up the stairs that love has made and
looks out the window which hope has opened.

CHARLES H. SPURGEON

Faith, as the Bible defines it, is present-tense action.
Faith means being sure of what we hope for...now.
It means knowing something is real, this moment,
all around you, even when you don't see it.
Great faith isn't the ability to believe long and
far into the misty future. It's simply taking God
at His word and taking the next step.

JONI EARECKSON TADA

*Faith is being sure of what we hope
for and certain of what we do not see.*

HEBREWS 11:1 NIV

Faithfulness Extended

Remember your promise to me,
for it is my only hope.
Your promise revives me;
it comforts me in all my troubles....
I meditate on your age-old regulations;
O LORD, they comfort me....
Your decrees have been the theme of my songs
wherever I have lived.
I reflect at night on who you are, O LORD;
therefore, I obey your instructions....
Your eternal word, O LORD,
stands firm in heaven.
Your faithfulness extends to every generation,
as enduring as the earth you created.
Your regulations remain true to this day.

PSALM 119:49–50, 52, 54–55, 89–91 NLT

Swim through your troubles. Run to the promises,
they are our Lord's branches hanging over the water
so that His children may take a grip of them.

SAMUEL RUTHERFORD

For great is your love, reaching to the heavens;
your faithfulness reaches to the skies.
Be exalted, O God, above the heavens;
let your glory be over all the earth.

PSALM 57:10–11 NIV

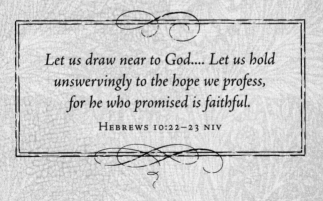

*Let us draw near to God.... Let us hold
unswervingly to the hope we profess,
for he who promised is faithful.*

HEBREWS 10:22–23 NIV

Enfolded in Peace

I will let God's peace infuse every part of today.
As the chaos swirls and life's demands pull
at me on all sides, I will breathe in God's peace
that surpasses all understanding.
He has promised that He would set within me
a peace too deeply planted to be affected
by unexpected or exhausting demands.

Calm me, O Lord, as you stilled the storm,
Still me, O Lord, keep me from harm.
Let all the tumult within me cease,
Enfold me, Lord, in your peace.

CELTIC TRADITIONAL

Peace is a margin of power around our daily need.
Peace is a consciousness of springs too deep
for earthly droughts to dry up.

HARRY EMERSON FOSDICK

The light of God surrounds me;
The love of God enfolds me;
The power of God protects me;
The presence of God watches over me.
Wherever I am, God is.

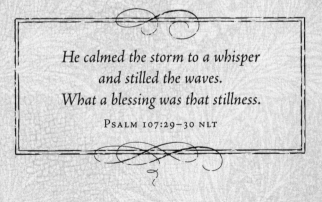

He calmed the storm to a whisper
and stilled the waves.
What a blessing was that stillness.

PSALM 107:29–30 NLT

Shining Promises

We do not know how this is true—
where would faith be if we did?—
but we do know that all things
that happen are full of shining seed.
Light is sown for us—not darkness.

The rain and snow come down from the heavens
and stay on the ground to water the earth.
They cause the grain to grow,
producing seed for the farmer
and bread for the hungry.
It is the same with my word.
I send it out, and it always produces fruit.
It will accomplish all I want it to,
and it will prosper everywhere I send it.

ISAIAH 55:10–11 NLT

Our feelings do not affect God's facts. They may blow up, like clouds, and cover the eternal things that we do most truly believe. We may not see the shining of the promises—but they still shine! [His strength] is not for one moment less because of our human weakness.

AMY CARMICHAEL

God's ways seem dark, but soon or late,
They touch the shining hills of day.

JOHN GREENLEAF WHITTIER

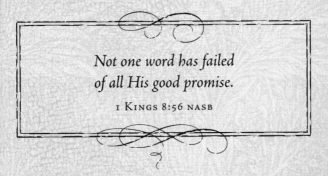

*Not one word has failed
of all His good promise.*

1 KINGS 8:56 NASB

Trust God's Heart

He writes in characters too grand
for our short sight to understand.
We catch but broken strokes
and try to fathom all the withered hopes
Of death, of life,
the endless war, the useless strife....
But there, with larger, clearer sight, we shall see this:
His way was right.

JOHN OXENHAM

Trust God where you cannot trace Him.
Do not try to penetrate the cloud He brings
over you; rather look to the bow that is on it.
The mystery is God's; the promise is yours.

JOHN MACDUFF

Wait upon God's strengthening, and say to Him,
"O Lord, You have been our refuge in all
generations." Trust in Him who has placed this
burden on you. What you yourself cannot bear,
bear with the help of God who is all-powerful.

BONIFACE

In those times I can't seem to find God, I rest in the
assurance He knows how to find me.

NEVA COYLE

Lord, You have been our dwelling place....
Even from everlasting to everlasting,
You are God.

PSALM 90:1–2 NASB

Countless Beauties

Forbid that I should walk through Thy beautiful
world with unseeing eyes:
Forbid that the lure of the market-place should ever
entirely steal my heart away from the love of the
open acres and the green trees:
Forbid that under the low roof of workshop or
office or study I should ever forget Thy great
overarching sky.

JOHN BAILLIE

Our Creator would never have made such lovely
days, and given us the deep hearts to enjoy them,
above and beyond all thought, unless we were
meant to be immortal.

NATHANIEL HAWTHORNE

May God give you eyes to see beauty
only the heart can understand.

From the world we see, hear, and touch,
we behold inspired visions that reveal God's glory.
In the sun's light, we catch warm rays of grace
and glimpse His eternal design. In the birds' song,
we hear His voice and it reawakens our desire
for Him. At the wind's touch, we feel His Spirit
and sense our eternal existence.

All the world is an utterance of the Almighty.
Its countless beauties, its exquisite adaptations,
all speak to you of Him.

PHILLIPS BROOKS

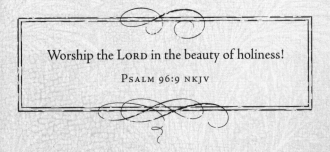

Worship the LORD in the beauty of holiness!

PSALM 96:9 NKJV

Safe in His Dwelling

The Lord is my light and my salvation—
whom shall I fear?
The Lord is the stronghold of my life—
of whom shall I be afraid?...
One thing I ask of the Lord,
this is what I seek:
that I may dwell in the house of the Lord
all the days of my life,
to gaze upon the beauty of the Lord
and to seek him in his temple.
For in the day of trouble
he will keep me safe in his dwelling;
he will hide me in the shelter of his tabernacle
and set me high upon a rock....
Hear my voice when I call, O Lord;
be merciful to me and answer me.
My heart says of you, "Seek his face!"
Your face, Lord, I will seek.

PSALM 27:1, 4–5, 7–8 NIV

The God who holds
the whole world in His hands
wraps Himself in the splendor
of the sun's light and
walks among the clouds.

Leave behind your fear and dwell
on the lovingkindness of God,
that you may recover
by gazing on Him.

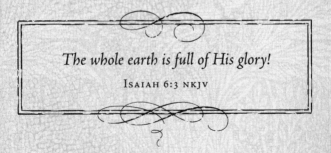

The whole earth is full of His glory!

ISAIAH 6:3 NKJV

Your Personal God

Don't be afraid, I've redeemed you.
I've called your name. You're mine.
When you're in over your head,
I'll be there with you.
When you're in rough waters, you will not go down.
When you're between a rock and a hard place,
it won't be a dead end—
Because I am God, your personal God,
The Holy of Israel, your Savior.
I paid a huge price for you...!
That's how much you mean to me!
That's how much I love you!

ISAIAH 43:1–4 MSG

Do not be afraid to enter the cloud that
is settling down on your life. God is in it.
The other side is radiant with His glory.

L. B. COWMAN

Let him who walks in the dark,
who has no light,
trust in the name of the LORD
and rely on his God.

ISAIAH 50:10 NIV

Our days are filled with tiny golden minutes with
eternity in them. Our lives are immortal. One
thousand years from this day you will be more alive
than you are at this moment. There is a future life
with God for those who put their trust in Him.

BILLY GRAHAM

If God be for us, who can be against us?

ROMANS 8:31 KJV

Waiting Quietly

The best reason to pray is that God is really there.
In praying, our unbelief gradually starts to melt.
God moves smack into the middle of even an
ordinary day.... Prayer is a matter of keeping at
it.... Thunderclaps and lightning flashes are very
unlikely. It is well to start small and quietly.

EMILY GRIFFIN

In waiting we begin to get in touch with the
rhythms of life—stillness and action, listening and
decision. They are the rhythms of God. It is in
the everyday and the commonplace that we learn
patience, acceptance, and contentment.

RICHARD J. FOSTER

God makes a promise—faith believes it, hope anticipates it, patience quietly awaits it.

When you get into a tight place and everything goes against you, till it seems as though you could not hang on a minute longer, never give up then, for that is just the place and time that the tide will turn.

HARRIET BEECHER STOWE

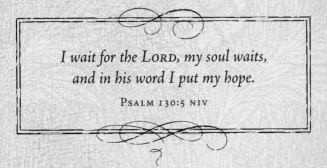

I wait for the LORD, my soul waits,
and in his word I put my hope.

PSALM 130:5 NIV

Pour Out Your Heart

The simple fact of being...in the presence of the
Lord and of showing Him all that I think, feel,
sense, and experience, without trying to hide
anything, must please Him. Somehow, somewhere,
I know that He loves me, even though I do not feel
that love as I can feel a human embrace,
even though I do not hear a voice as I hear human
words of consolation.... God is greater than my
senses, greater than my thoughts, greater than
my heart. I do believe that He touches me
in places that are unknown even to myself.

HENRI J. M. NOUWEN

Genuine heart-hunger, accompanied
by sincere seeking after eternal values,
does not go unrewarded.

JUSTINE KNIGHT

Lord Jesus Christ...
May I know You more clearly,
Love You more dearly
And follow You more nearly
Day by day. Amen.

Richard of Chichester

Pour out your heart to God your Father.
He understands you better than you do.

My soul longed and even yearned for the
courts of the Lord;
My heart and my flesh sing for joy
to the living God.

Psalm 84:2 NASB

He Restores My Soul

The LORD is my shepherd, I shall not be in want.
He makes me lie down in green pastures,
he leads me beside quiet waters,
he restores my soul.
He guides me in paths of righteousness
for his name's sake.
Even though I walk through the
valley of the shadow of death,
I will fear no evil,
for you are with me;
your rod and your staff,
they comfort me.
You prepare a table before me
in the presence of my enemies.
You anoint my head with oil;
my cup overflows.
Surely goodness and love will follow me
all the days of my life,
and I will dwell in the house of the LORD
forever.

PSALM 23:1-6 NIV

The purpose of grace is primarily
to restore our relationship with God....
This is what all the work of grace aims at—
an ever deeper knowledge of God,
and an ever closer fellowship with Him.

J. I. PACKER

You have made us for Thyself, O Lord;
and our hearts are restless until
they find rest in Thee.

AUGUSTINE

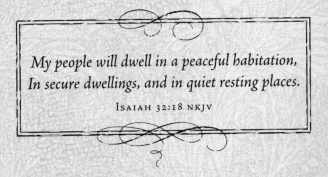

My people will dwell in a peaceful habitation,
In secure dwellings, and in quiet resting places.

ISAIAH 32:18 NKJV

Always There

We need never shout across the spaces to
an absent God. He is nearer than our own soul,
closer than our most secret thoughts.

A. W. TOZER

God is the sunshine that warms us, the rain
that melts the frost and waters the young plants.
The presence of God is a climate of strong and
bracing love, always there.

JOAN ARNOLD

God is always present in the temple of your heart...
His home. And when you come in to meet Him
there, you find that it is the one place of deep
satisfaction where every longing is met.

Always be in a state of expectancy, and see that you leave room for God to come in as He likes.

OSWALD CHAMBERS

A living, loving God can and does make His presence felt, can and does speak to us in the silence of our hearts, can and does warm and caress us till we no longer doubt that He is near, that He is here.

BRENNAN MANNING

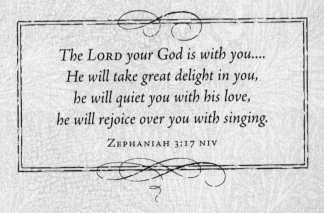

The LORD your God is with you....
He will take great delight in you,
he will quiet you with his love,
he will rejoice over you with singing.

ZEPHANIAH 3:17 NIV

His Imprint

The God of the universe—the One
who created everything and holds it all
in His hand—created each of us in His image,
to bear His likeness, His imprint. It is only
when Christ dwells within our hearts,
radiating the pure light of His love through
our humanity that we discover who we are
and what we were intended to be.

In the very beginning it was God who formed us
by His Word. He made us in His own image.
God was spirit and He gave us a spirit
so that He could come into us and
mingle His own life with our life.

MADAME JEANNE GUYON

You are a little less than angels, crown of creation,
image of God. Each person is a revelation,
a transfiguration, a waiting for Him
to manifest Himself.

EDWARD FARRELL

Made in His image, we can have real meaning,
and we can have real knowledge through what
He has communicated to us.

FRANCIS SCHAEFFER

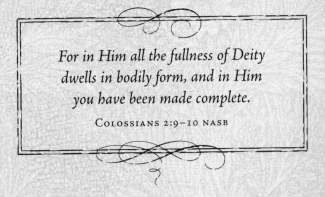

*For in Him all the fullness of Deity
dwells in bodily form, and in Him
you have been made complete.*

COLOSSIANS 2:9–10 NASB

Rest in Him

My soul finds rest in God alone;
my salvation comes from him.
He alone is my rock and my salvation;
he is my fortress, I will never be shaken....
My salvation and my honor depend on God;
he is my mighty rock, my refuge.
Trust in him at all times, O people;
pour out your hearts to him,
for God is our refuge....
One thing God has spoken,
two things have I heard:
that you, O God, are strong,
and that you, O Lord, are loving.

PSALM 62:1–2, 7–8, 11–12 NIV

Joy comes from knowing God loves me
and knows who I am and where I'm going...
that my future is secure as I rest in Him.

DR. JAMES DOBSON

When God finds a soul that rests in Him
and is not easily moved...to this same soul
He gives the joy of His presence.

CATHERINE OF GENOA

Let the beloved of the LORD rest secure in him,
for he shields him all day long,
and the one the Lord loves rests between
his shoulders.

DEUTERONOMY 33:12 NIV

Rest in the LORD, and wait patiently for him.

PSALM 37:7 KJV

An Invitation

Come, all you who are thirsty,
come to the waters; and you who
have no money, come, buy and eat!
Come, buy wine and milk
without money and without cost.
Why spend money on what is not bread,
and your labor on what does not satisfy?
Listen, listen to me, and eat what is good,
and your soul will delight in the richest of fare.
Give ear and come to me;
hear me, that your soul may live.

ISAIAH 55:1–3 NIV

[God] is looking for people who will come
in simple dependence upon His grace,
and rest in simple faith upon His greatness.
At this very moment, He's looking at you.

JACK HAYFORD

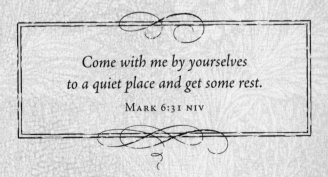

Are you tired? Worn out? Burned out on religion?
Come to me. Get away with me and
you'll recover your life. I'll show you how
to take a real rest. Walk with me and work
with me—watch how I do it. Learn the unforced
rhythms of grace. I won't lay anything heavy
or ill-fitting on you. Keep company with me
and you'll learn to live freely and lightly.

MATTHEW 11:28–30 MSG

Come with me by yourselves
to a quiet place and get some rest.

MARK 6:31 NIV

A River of Delights

Your love, O LORD, reaches to the heavens,
your faithfulness to the skies.
Your righteousness is like the mighty mountains,
your justice like the great deep....
How priceless is your unfailing love!
Both high and low among men
find refuge in the shadow of your wings.
They feast on the abundance of your house;
you give them drink from your river of delights.
For with you is the fountain of life;
in your light we see light.

PSALM 36:5–9 NIV

What extraordinary delight we find
in the presence of God. He draws us in,
His welcome so fresh and inviting.

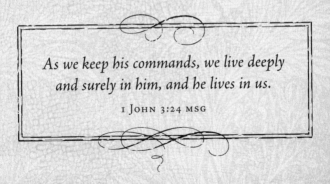

O the pure delight of a single hour
that before Thy throne I spend,
When I kneel in prayer, and with Thee, my God,
I commune as friend with friend!

FANNY J. CROSBY

God's love is like a river springing up
in the Divine Substance and flowing endlessly
through His creation, filling all things with life
and goodness and strength.

THOMAS MERTON

As we keep his commands, we live deeply
and surely in him, and he lives in us.

1 JOHN 3:24 MSG

A Safe Journey

He rescues you from hidden traps,
shields you from deadly hazards.
His huge outstretched arms protect you—
under them you're perfectly safe;
his arms fend off all harm.
Fear nothing—not wild wolves in the night,
not flying arrows in the day,
not disease that prowls through the darkness,
not disaster that erupts at high noon....
"If you'll hold on to me for dear life," says GOD,
"I'll get you out of any trouble.
I'll give you the best of care
if you'll only get to know and trust me.
Call me and I'll answer, be at your side
in bad times."

PSALM 91:3–6, 14–15 MSG

May your life become one of glad
and unending praise to the Lord as you
journey through this world.

TERESA OF AVILA

God has not promised us an easy journey,
but He has promised us a safe journey.

WILLIAM C. MILLER

It is God to whom and with whom we travel,
and while He is the End of our journey,
He is also at every stopping place.

ELISABETH ELLIOT

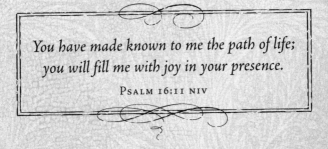

*You have made known to me the path of life;
you will fill me with joy in your presence.*

PSALM 16:11 NIV

Made for Joy

Our hearts were made for joy. Our hearts were
made to enjoy the One who created them.
Too deeply planted to be much affected by
the ups and downs of life, this joy is a
knowing and a being known by our Creator.
He sets our hearts alight with radiant joy.

WENDY MOORE

You will go out in joy
and be led forth in peace;
the mountains and hills
will burst into song before you,
and all the trees of the field
will clap their hands.

ISAIAH 55:12 NIV

If one is joyful, it means that one is faithfully living for God, and that nothing else counts; and if one gives joy to others one is doing God's work. With joy without and joy within, all is well.

JANET ERSKINE STUART

Live for today but hold your hands open to tomorrow. Anticipate the future and its changes with joy. There is a seed of God's love in every event, every circumstance, every unpleasant situation in which you may find yourself.

BARBARA JOHNSON

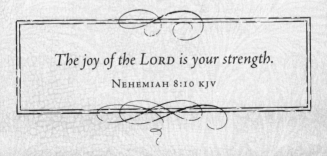

The joy of the LORD is your strength.

NEHEMIAH 8:10 KJV

Nothing but Grace

There is nothing but God's grace. We walk
upon it; we breathe it; we live and die by it;
it makes the nails and axles of the universe.

ROBERT LOUIS STEVENSON

The "air" which our souls need also envelops
all of us at all times and on all sides. God
is round about us in Christ on every hand,
with many-sided and all-sufficient grace.
All we need to do is to open our hearts.

OLE HALLESBY

Jesus Christ opens wide the doors of the treasure
house of God's promises, and bids us go in and
take with boldness the riches that are ours.

CORRIE TEN BOOM

Grace is no stationary thing, it is ever becoming.
It is flowing straight out of God's heart. Grace does
nothing but re-form and convey God. Grace makes
the soul conformable to the will of God. God, the
ground of the soul, and grace go together.

MEISTER ECKHART

Grace and gratitude belong together like
heaven and earth. Grace evokes gratitude
like the voice an echo. Gratitude follows grace
as thunder follows lightning.

KARL BARTH

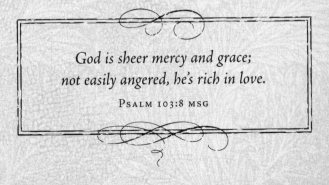

God is sheer mercy and grace;
not easily angered, he's rich in love.

PSALM 103:8 MSG

God's Eternal Love

The LORD is like a father to his children,
tender and compassionate to those who fear him.
For he knows how weak we are;
he remembers we are only dust.
Our days on earth are like grass;
like wildflowers, we bloom and die.
The wind blows, and we are gone—
as though we had never been here.
But the love of the LORD remains forever....
The LORD has made the heavens his throne;
from there he rules over everything.

PSALM 103:13–17, 19 NLT

The reason we can dare to risk loving others is
that "God has for Christ's sake loved us." Think
of it! We are loved eternally, totally, individually,
unreservedly! Nothing can take God's love away.

GLORIA GAITHER

*A*mid the ebb and flow of the passing world,
our God remains unmoved,
and His throne endures forever.

ROBERT COLEMAN

I am wholly His; I am peculiarly His;
I am universally His; I am eternally His.

THOMAS BENTON BROOKS

*Great is his love toward us,
and the faithfulness of the* LORD
endures forever.

PSALM 117:2 NIV

Contemplating God

We are so preciously loved by God that we cannot
even comprehend it. No created being can ever
know how much and how sweetly and tenderly
God loves them. It is only with the help of His
grace that we are able to persevere in spiritual
contemplation with endless wonder at His high,
surpassing, immeasurable love which our
Lord in His goodness has for us.

JULIAN OF NORWICH

Contemplation is nothing else but a
secret, peaceful, and loving infusion of God,
which, if admitted, will set the soul
on fire with the spirit of love.

JOHN OF THE CROSS

Take a moment to consider the awesome reality
that the God who spoke and created the universe
is now speaking to you. If Jesus could speak
and raise the dead, calm a storm...and heal the
incurable, then what effect might a word from
Him have upon your life?

HENRY T. BLACKABY

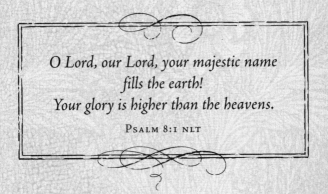

*O Lord, our Lord, your majestic name
fills the earth!
Your glory is higher than the heavens.*

PSALM 8:1 NLT

He Carries Our Sorrows

There is a sacredness in tears.
They are not the mark of weakness,
but of power. They speak more eloquently
than ten thousand tongues. They are
the messengers of overwhelming grief,
of deep contrition, and of unspeakable love.

WASHINGTON IRVING

Your tears are precious to God. They are like
stained-glass windows in the darkness, whose true
beauty is revealed only when there is a light within.

When Jesus...confides to us that
He is "acquainted with Grief,"
we listen, for that also is an
Acquaintance of our own.

EMILY DICKINSON

The sun will no more be your light by day,
nor will the brightness of the moon shine on you,
for the LORD will be your everlasting light,
and your God will be your glory.
Your sun will never set again,
and your moon will wane no more;
the LORD will be your everlasting light,
and your days of sorrow will end.

ISAIAH 60:19–20 NIV

A teardrop on earth summons the King of Heaven.

CHARLES R. SWINDOLL

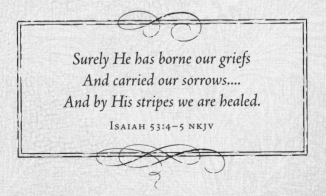

*Surely He has borne our griefs
And carried our sorrows....
And by His stripes we are healed.*

ISAIAH 53:4–5 NKJV

Powerful Love

I pray that out of his glorious riches he may
strengthen you with power through his Spirit in
your inner being, so that Christ may dwell in your
hearts through faith. And I pray that you, being
rooted and established in love, may have power,
together with all the saints, to grasp how wide and
long and high and deep is the love of Christ,
and to know this love that surpasses knowledge—
that you may be filled to the measure
of all the fullness of God.

Now to him who is able to do immeasurably
more than all we ask or imagine, according to his
power that is at work within us, to him be glory
in the church and in Christ Jesus throughout all
generations, for ever and ever! Amen.

EPHESIANS 3:16–21 NIV

We have a Father in heaven
who is almighty, who loves His children
as He loves His only-begotten Son,
and whose very joy and delight
it is to...help them at all times
and under all circumstances.

GEORGE MÜELLER

As high as heaven is over the earth,
so strong is his love to those who fear him.

PSALM 103:11 MSG

I Lift Up My Eyes

I lift up mine eyes to the quiet hills,
and my heart to the Father's throne;
in all my ways, to the end of days,
the Lord will preserve His own.

TIMOTHY DUDLEY-SMITH

Where can I go from your Spirit?
Where can I flee from your presence?
If I go up to the heavens, you are there;
if I make my bed in the depths, you are there.
If I rise on the wings of the dawn,
if I settle on the far side of the sea,
even there your hand will guide me,
your right hand will hold me fast.

PSALM 139:7–10 NIV

You, O LORD, are a shield for me,
My glory and the One who lifts up my head.
I cried to the LORD, and He heard me
from His holy hill.

PSALM 3:3–4 NKJV

Know by the light of faith that God is present,
and be content with directing all your
actions toward Him.

BROTHER LAWRENCE

I lift my eyes to you,
O God, enthroned in heaven.
We look to the LORD our God for his mercy.

PSALM 123:1–2 NLT

Showers of Blessings

Bless the LORD, O my soul;
And all that is within me, bless His holy name!
Bless the LORD, O my soul,
And forget not all His benefits:
Who forgives all your iniquities,
Who heals all your diseases,
Who redeems your life from destruction,
Who crowns you with lovingkindness
and tender mercies,
Who satisfies your mouth with good things,
So that your youth is renewed like the eagle's.

PSALM 103:1–5 NKJV

God, who is love—who is, if I may say it this way,
made out of love—simply cannot help but shed
blessing on blessing upon us.

HANNAH WHITALL SMITH

God is waiting for us to come to Him with our
needs.... God's throne room is always open....
Every single believer in the whole world could
walk into the throne room all at one time,
and it would not even be crowded.

CHARLES STANLEY

Lift up your eyes. Your heavenly Father waits to
bless you—in inconceivable ways to make your life
what you never dreamed it could be.

ANNE ORTLUND

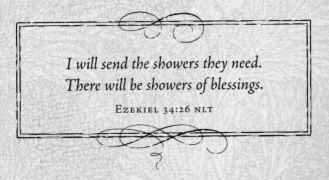

*I will send the showers they need.
There will be showers of blessings.*

EZEKIEL 34:26 NLT

Grace for Trials

God has not promised skies always blue,
flower-strewn pathways all our lives through;
God has not promised sun without rain,
joy without sorrow, peace without pain.
But God has promised strength for the day,
rest for the labor, light for the way,
grace for the trials, help from above,
unfailing sympathy, undying love.

ANNIE JOHNSON FLINT

Trials have no value or intrinsic meaning in
themselves. It's the way we respond to those trials
that makes all the difference.

JONI EARECKSON TADA

Character cannot be developed in ease and quiet.
Only through experience of trial and suffering can
the soul be strengthened.

HELEN KELLER

We also rejoice in our sufferings, because we know that suffering produces perseverance; perseverance, character; and character, hope. And hope does not disappoint us, because God has poured out his love into our hearts by the Holy Spirit, whom he has given us.

ROMANS 5:3–5 NIV

After winter comes the summer. After night comes the dawn. And after every storm, there comes clear, open skies.

SAMUEL RUTHERFORD

They that sow in tears shall reap in joy.

PSALM 126:5 KJV

Light in the Darkness

There is not enough darkness in all the world to put out the light of one small candle.... In moments of discouragement, defeat, or even despair, there are always certain things to cling to. Little things usually: remembered laughter, the face of a sleeping child, a tree in the wind—in fact, any reminder of something deeply felt or dearly loved. No one is so poor as not to have many of these small candles. When they are lighted, darkness goes away and a touch of wonder remains.

ARTHUR GORDON

One taper lights a thousand,
Yet shines as it has shone;
And the humblest light may kindle
A brighter than its own.

HEZEKIAN BUTTERWORTH

It should fill us with joy, that infinite wisdom
guides the affairs of the world...that infinite
wisdom directs every event, brings order out
of confusion, and light out of darkness, and,
to those who love God, causes all things,
whatever be their present aspect and apparent
tendency, to work together for good.

J. L. Dagg

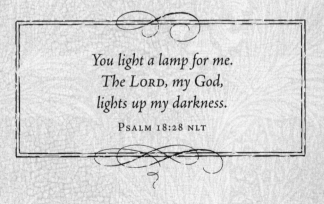

You light a lamp for me.
The Lord, my God,
lights up my darkness.

Psalm 18:28 NLT

Comfort Sweet

He is the Source. Of everything.
Strength for your day. Wisdom for your task.
Comfort for your soul. Grace for your battle.
Provision for each need.

JACK HAYFORD

There is a place of comfort sweet
Near to the heart of God,
A place where we our Savior meet,
Near to the heart of God....
Hold us who wait before Thee
Near to the heart of God.

CLELAND B. MCAFEE

God comforts. He lays His right hand on the
wounded soul...and He says, as if that one were
the only soul in all the universe: O greatly beloved,
fear not: peace be unto thee.

AMY CARMICHAEL

Every now and again take a good look at something not made with hands—a mountain, a star, the turn of a stream. There will come to you wisdom and patience and solace and, above all, the assurance that you are not alone in the world.

SIDNEY LOVETT

It is such a comfort to drop the tangles of life into God's hands and leave them there.

L. B. COWMAN

Rejoice, be made complete, be comforted... live in peace; and the God of love and peace will be with you.

2 CORINTHIANS 13:11 NASB

Intercession

And the Holy Spirit helps us in our weakness.
For example, we don't know what God wants us
to pray for. But the Holy Spirit prays for us with
groanings that cannot be expressed in words. And
the Father who knows all hearts knows what the
Spirit is saying, for the Spirit pleads for us believers
in harmony with God's own will. And we know
that God causes everything to work together for
the good of those who love God and are called
according to his purpose for them.

ROMANS 8:26–28 NLT

When life tumbles in and problems
overwhelm us...how reassuring it is to know
that the Spirit makes intercession for us!

HAZEL C. LEE

Prayer is such an ordinary, everyday, mundane thing. Certainly, people who pray are no more saints than the rest of us. Rather, they are people who want to share a life with God, to love and be loved, to speak and to listen, to work and to be at rest in the presence of God.

ROBERTA BONDI

If you don't know what you're doing, pray to the Father. He loves to help.

JAMES 1:5 MSG

The Beauty of God's Peace

Let not your heart be troubled: ye believe in God, believe also in me. In my Father's house are many mansions: if it were not so, I would have told you. I go to prepare a place for you. And if I go and prepare a place for you, I will come again, and receive you unto myself; that where I am, there ye may be also....

I will not leave you comfortless: I will come to you.... Peace I leave with you, my peace I give unto you: not as the world giveth, give I unto you. Let not your heart be troubled, neither let it be afraid.

JOHN 14:1–3, 18, 27 KJV

Drop Thy still dews of quietness
till all our strivings cease;
take from our souls the strain and stress,
and let our ordered lives confess
the beauty of Thy peace.

JOHN GREENLEAF WHITTIER

May the God of love and peace set your heart
at rest and speed you on your journey.

RAYMOND OF PENYAFORT

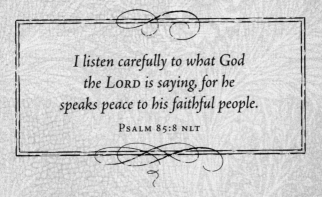

*I listen carefully to what God
the LORD is saying, for he
speaks peace to his faithful people.*

PSALM 85:8 NLT

Seek the Lord

In extravagance of soul we seek His face. In
generosity of heart, we glean His gentle touch. In
excessiveness of spirit, we love Him and His love
comes back to us a hundredfold.

TRICIA MCCARY RHODES

The God who made the world and everything in it
is the Lord of heaven and earth.... He himself gives
all men life and breath and everything else....
God did this so that men would seek him and
perhaps reach out for him and find him, though
he is not far from each one of us. "For in him
we live, and move, and have our being."

ACTS 17:24–25, 27–28 NIV

I have sought Thy nearness;
With all my heart have I called Thee,
And going out to meet Thee
I found Thee coming toward me.

YEHUDA HALEVI

God is not an elusive dream or a phantom
to chase, but a divine person to know. He does
not avoid us, but seeks us. When we seek Him,
the contact is instantaneous.

NEVA COYLE

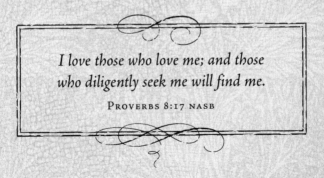

*I love those who love me; and those
who diligently seek me will find me.*

PROVERBS 8:17 NASB

Every Need

"So do not fear, for I am with you;
do not be dismayed, for I am your God.
I will strengthen you and help you;
I will uphold you with my righteous right hand....
For I am the LORD, your God,
who takes hold of your right hand
and says to you, do not fear....
for I myself will help you," declares the LORD....
I will make rivers flow on barren heights,
and springs within the valleys.
I will turn the desert into pools of water,
and the parched ground into springs.

ISAIAH 41:10, 13–14, 18 NIV

Jesus Christ has brought every need...every hope
of ours before God. He accompanies us and
brings us into the presence of God.

DIETRICH BONHOEFFER

God wants nothing from us
except our needs, and these furnish Him
with room to display His bounty
when He supplies them freely....
Not what I have, but what I do not have,
is the first point of contact between
my soul and God.

CHARLES H. SPURGEON

*My God is changeless in his love for me
and he will come and help me.*

PSALM 59:10 TLB

God Is Our Refuge

Hear my cry, O God;
Give heed to my prayer.
From the end of the earth
I call to You when my heart is faint;
Lead me to the rock that is higher than I.
For You have been a refuge for me,
A tower of strength against the enemy.
Let me dwell in Your tent forever;
Let me take refuge in the shelter of Your wings.

PSALM 61:1–4 NASB

Beneath God's watchful eye
His saints securely dwell;
That Hand which bears all nature up
Shall guard His children well.

WILLIAM COWPER

When God has become...our refuge
and our fortress, then we can reach out
to Him in the midst of a broken world
and feel at home while still on the way.

HENRI J. M. NOUWEN

Children of the heavenly Father
Safely in His bosom gather;
Nestling bird nor star in heaven
Such a refuge e'er was given.

CAROLINA SANDELL BERG

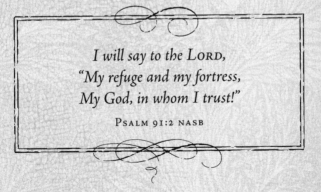

*I will say to the LORD,
"My refuge and my fortress,
My God, in whom I trust!"*

PSALM 91:2 NASB

Perfect Peace

Trials...may come in abundance. But they cannot
penetrate into the sanctuary of the soul when it is
settled in God, and we may dwell in perfect peace.

HANNAH WHITALL SMITH

God cannot give us a happiness and peace
apart from Himself, because it is not there.
There is no such thing.

C. S. LEWIS

What a friend we have in Jesus,
All our sins and griefs to bear;
What a privilege to carry
Everything to God in prayer.
O, what peace we often forfeit,
O, what needless pain we bear,
All because we do not carry
Everything to God in prayer.

JOSEPH M. SCRIVEN

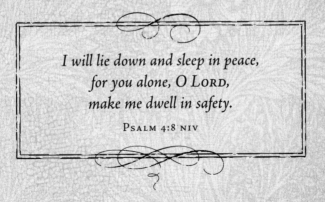

Night by night I will lie down
and sleep in the thought of God.

WILLIAM MOUNTFORD

Unceasing Prayer has a way of speaking peace
to the chaos. Our fractured and fragmented
activities begin focusing around a new Center
of Reference. We experience peace, stillness,
serenity, firmness of life orientation.

RICHARD J. FOSTER

I will lie down and sleep in peace,
for you alone, O LORD,
make me dwell in safety.

PSALM 4:8 NIV

Life of Faith

Our Heavenly Father...wants us to
reach up and take His hand, but
He doesn't want us to *ever* let go.
In fact, His desire is that we become
more and *more* dependent upon Him
for every step. That's because He wants to
take us to places we've never been.
To heights we can't even imagine....
God always requires the first step to be ours.
In order to take that first step, we must
look into the face of God, reach up
and take His hand, and say, "Lead me
in the path You have for me, Lord.
From this day on I want to walk with You."

STORMIE OMARTIAN

Living a life of faith means never knowing where you are being led. But it does mean loving and knowing the One who is leading. It is literally a life of faith, not of understanding and reason—a life of knowing Him who calls us to go.

OSWALD CHAMBERS

Faith is to believe what we do not see; and the reward of this faith is to see what we believe.

AUGUSTINE

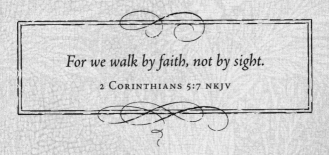

For we walk by faith, not by sight.

2 CORINTHIANS 5:7 NKJV

Faithful Guide

Guidance is a sovereign act. Not merely does God will to guide us by showing us His way...whatever mistakes we may make, we shall come safely home. Slippings and strayings there will be, no doubt, but the everlasting arms are beneath us; we shall be caught, rescued, restored. This is God's promise; this is how good He is. And our self-distrust, while keeping us humble, must not cloud the joy with which we lean on our faithful covenant God.

J. I. PACKER

Heaven often seems distant and unknown,
but if he who made the road...is our guide,
we need not fear to lose the way.

HENRY VAN DYKE

We are of such value to God that He came to live among us...and to guide us home. He will go to any length to seek us, even to being lifted high upon the cross to draw us back to Himself. We can only respond by loving God for His love.

CATHERINE OF SIENNA

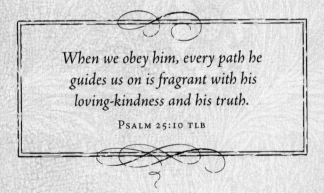

When we obey him, every path he guides us on is fragrant with his loving-kindness and his truth.

PSALM 25:10 TLB

Hope in God

Why are you in despair, O my soul?
And why have you become disturbed within me?
Hope in God, for I shall again praise Him
For the help of His presence.
O my God, my soul is in despair within me;
Therefore I remember You....
Deep calls to deep at the sound of Your waterfalls;
All Your breakers and Your waves have
rolled over me.
The LORD will command His lovingkindness
in the daytime;
And His song will be with me in the night,
A prayer to the God of my life.

PSALM 42:5–8 NASB

Hope is faith holding out its hands in the dark.

GEORGE ILES

Life is what we are alive to. It is not length but breadth.... Be alive to...goodness, kindness, purity, love, history, poetry, music, flowers, stars, God, and eternal hope.

MALTBIE D. BABCOCK

You are never alone. In your heart of hearts, in the place where no two people are ever alike, Christ is waiting for you. And what you never dared hope for springs to life.

ROGER OF TAIZÉ

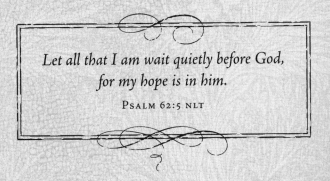

Let all that I am wait quietly before God, for my hope is in him.

PSALM 62:5 NLT

Settled in Solitude

Solitude liberates us from entanglements by carving out a space from which we can see ourselves and our situation before the Audience of One. Solitude provides the private place where we can take our bearings and so make God our North Star.

Os Guinness

We must drink deeply from the very Source the deep calm and peace of interior quietude and refreshment of God, allowing the pure water of divine grace to flow plentifully and unceasingly from the Source itself.

Mother Teresa

Whoever drinks of the water that I will give him shall never thirst; but the water that I will give him will become in him a well of water springing up to eternal life.

John 4:14 NASB

Don't ever let yourself get so busy that you miss those little but important extras in life—the beauty of a day...the smile of a friend...the serenity of a quiet moment alone. For it is often life's smallest pleasures and gentlest joys that make the biggest and most lasting difference.

Settle yourself in solitude and you will come upon Him in yourself.

TERESA OF AVILA

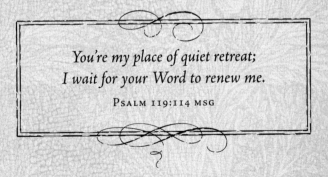

You're my place of quiet retreat;
I wait for your Word to renew me.

PSALM 119:114 MSG

God Understands

He heals the brokenhearted
and binds up their wounds.
He determines the number of the stars
and calls them each by name.
Great is our Lord and mighty in power;
his understanding has no limit....
The LORD delights in those who fear him,
who put their hope in his unfailing love.

PSALM 147:3–5, 11 NIV

God understands our prayers even when we can't
find the words to say them.

God possesses infinite knowledge and an awareness
which is uniquely His. At all times, even in the
midst of any type of suffering, I can realize that
He knows, loves, watches, understands,
and more than that, He has a purpose.

BILLY GRAHAM

Bestow upon me, O Lord my God,
understanding to know You, diligence to seek You,
wisdom to find You, and a faithfulness
that may finally embrace You.

THOMAS AQUINAS

Everything God does is love—even when
we do not understand Him.

BASILEA SCHLINK

Trust in the LORD with all your heart;
And lean not on your own understanding;
In all your ways acknowledge Him,
And He shall direct your paths.

PROVERBS 3:5–6 NKJV

Sought and Found

It is God's will that we believe that we see Him
continually, though it seems to us that the sight be
only partial; and through this belief He makes us
always to gain more grace, for God wishes to be
seen, and He wishes to be sought, and He wishes
to be expected, and He wishes to be trusted.

JULIAN OF NORWICH

If you are seeking after God, you may be sure
of this: God is seeking you much more.
He is the Lover, and you are His beloved.
He has promised Himself to you.

JOHN OF THE CROSS

To seek God means first of all to let
yourself be found by Him.

God's nature is given me. His love is jealous for my
life. All His attributes are woven into the pattern of
my spirit. What a God is this! His life implanted in
every child. Thank you, Father, for this.

JIM ELLIOT

They who seek the throne of grace
Find that throne in every place;
If we live a life of prayer,
God is present everywhere.

OLIVER HOLDEN

*Seek the LORD your God, and you
will find him if you seek him with all
your heart and with all your soul.*

DEUTERONOMY 4:29 NIV

New Every Morning

Experience God in the breathless wonder and
startling beauty that is all around you. His sun
shines warm upon your face. His wind whispers in
the treetops. Like the first rays of morning light,
celebrate the start of each day with God.

WENDY MOORE

Those who have met God are not looking
for something—they have found it;
they are not searching for light—upon them
the Light has already shined.

A.W. TOZER

Always new. Always exciting. Always full of
promise. The mornings of our lives,
each a personal daily miracle!

GLORIA GAITHER

A quiet morning with a loving God puts the events
of the upcoming day into proper perspective.

JANETTE OKE

The sun...in its full glory, either at rising or setting—this, and many other like blessings we enjoy daily; and for the most of them, because they are so common, most men forget to pay their praises. But let not us.

IZAAK WALTON

Life begins each morning.... Each morning is the open door to a new world—new vistas, new aims, new tryings.

LEIGH MITCHELL HODGES

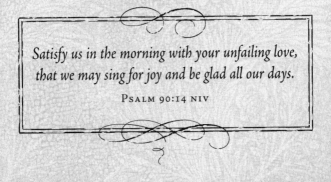

Satisfy us in the morning with your unfailing love, that we may sing for joy and be glad all our days.

PSALM 90:14 NIV

My Help

I lift up my eyes to the hills—
where does my help come from?
My help comes from the Lord,
the Maker of heaven and earth.
He will not let your foot slip—
he who watches over you will not slumber;
indeed, he who watches over Israel
will neither slumber nor sleep.
The Lord watches over you—
the Lord is your shade at your right hand;
the sun will not harm you by day,
nor the moon by night.
The Lord will keep you from all harm—
he will watch over your life;
the Lord will watch over your coming and going
both now and forevermore.

PSALM 121:1–8 KJV

We may not all reach God's ideal for us,
but with His help we may move in that
direction day by day as we relate every
detail of our lives to Him.

CAROL GISH

Be assured, if you walk with Him
and look to Him and expect help from Him,
He will never fail you.

GEORGE MÜELLER

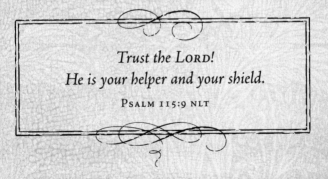

Trust the LORD!
He is your helper and your shield.

PSALM 115:9 NLT

Sweet Hour of Prayer

Sweet hour of prayer, sweet hour of prayer,
That calls me from a world of care,
And bids me at my Father's throne,
Make all my wants and wishes known!
In seasons of distress and grief,
My soul has often found relief,
And oft escaped the tempter's snare
By Thy return, sweet hour of prayer.

WILLIAM W. WALFORD

If we knew how to listen, we would hear Him
speaking to us. For God does speak.... If we knew
how to listen to God, if we knew how to look
around us, our whole life would become prayer.

MICHAEL QUOIST

All good meditative prayer is a conversion
of our entire self to God.

THOMAS MERTON

Our Father in heaven,
Hallowed be Your name.
Your kingdom come.
Your will be done
On earth as it is in heaven.
Give us this day our daily bread.
And forgive us our debts,
As we forgive our debtors.
And do not lead us into temptation,
But deliver us from the evil one.
For Yours is the kingdom
and the power and the glory forever.
Amen.

MATTHEW 6:9–13 NKJV

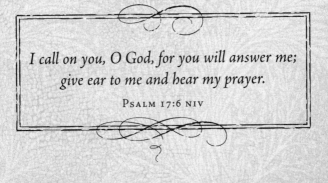

I call on you, O God, for you will answer me;
give ear to me and hear my prayer.

PSALM 17:6 NIV

Fresh Hope

I don't know, when I'm asking for something
here on earth, what is going on in the innermost
shrine of Heaven (I like to think about it, though).
I am sure of one thing: it is good. Because Jesus
is there. Jesus loves me. Jesus has gone into
that shrine on my behalf. The hope we have
is a living hope, an unassailable one.
We wait for it, in faith and patience.

ELISABETH ELLIOT

God...rekindles burned-out lives with fresh hope,
restoring dignity and respect to their lives—
a place in the sun!
For the very structures of earth are God's;
he has laid out his operations on a firm foundation.

1 SAMUEL 2:7–8 MSG

God specializes in things fresh and firsthand.
His plans for you this year may outshine those
of the past.... He's preparing to fill your days
with reasons to give Him praise.

JONI EARECKSON TADA

Within each of us, just waiting to blossom,
is the wonderful promise of all we can be.

*Let your unfailing love surround us, LORD,
for our hope is in you alone.*

PSALM 33:22 NLT

God Listens

God listens in compassion and love, just like we
do when our children come to us. He delights in
our presence. When we do this, we will discover
something of inestimable value. We will discover
that by praying we learn to pray.

RICHARD J. FOSTER

When we call on God, He bends down
His ear to listen, as a father bends down
to listen to his little child.

ELIZABETH CHARLES

God came to us because God wanted to join us
on the road, to listen to our story, and to help us
realize that we are not walking in circles but moving
toward the house of peace and joy.

HENRI J. M. NOUWEN

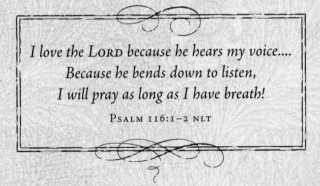

We come this morning—
Like empty pitchers to a full fountain,
With no merits of our own,
O Lord—open up a window of heaven...
And listen this morning.

JAMES WELDON JOHNSON

I love the LORD because he hears my voice....
Because he bends down to listen,
I will pray as long as I have breath!

PSALM 116:1–2 NLT

The Goodness of God

God never abandons anyone on whom He
has set His love; nor does Christ, the good
shepherd, ever lose track of His sheep.
How slow we are to believe in God as God,
sovereign, all-seeing and almighty! We need to
"wait upon the Lord" in meditations on His
majesty, till we find our strength renewed through
the writing of these things upon our hearts.

J. I. PACKER

God is the God of promise. He keeps His word,
even when that seems impossible.

COLIN URQUHART

The LORD longs to be gracious to you;
he rises to show you compassion.
For the LORD is a God of justice.
Blessed are all who wait for him!

ISAIAH 30:18 NIV

Be strong and courageous! Do not be afraid...! For the LORD your God will personally go ahead of you. He will neither fail you nor abandon you.

DEUTERONOMY 31:6 NLT

God is not merely good, but goodness;
goodness is not merely divine, but God.

C. S. LEWIS

The Lord's goodness surrounds us at every moment. I walk through it almost with difficulty, as through thick grass and flowers.

R. W. BARBER

The earth is full of the goodness of the LORD.

PSALM 33:5 KJV

Totally Aware

God is every moment totally aware of each
one of us. Totally aware in intense
concentration and love.... No one passes
through any area of life, happy or tragic,
without the attention of God with him.

EUGENIA PRICE

Because God is responsible for our welfare, we are
told to cast all our care upon Him, for He cares for
us. God says, "I'll take the burden—don't give it a
thought—leave it to Me." God is keenly aware that
we are dependent upon Him for life's necessities.

BILLY GRAHAM

You are God's created beauty and the focus
of His affection and delight.

JANET L. WEAVER SMITH

I am convinced that neither death nor life, neither angels nor demons, neither the present nor the future, nor any powers, neither height nor depth, nor anything else in all creation, will be able to separate us from the love of God that is in Christ Jesus our Lord.

ROMANS 8:38–39 NIV

Nothing can separate you from His love, absolutely nothing.... God is enough for time, and God is enough for eternity. God is enough!

HANNAH WHITALL SMITH

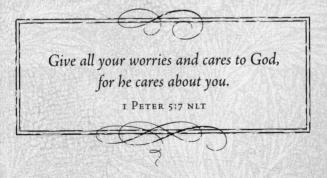

*Give all your worries and cares to God,
for he cares about you.*

1 PETER 5:7 NLT

God's Answers

A wise gardener plants his seeds,
then has the good sense not to dig them up
every few days to see if a crop is on the way.
Likewise, we must be patient as God
brings the answers...in His own good time.

QUIN SHERRER

Being able to bow in prayer as the day begins or
ends gives expression to the frustrations
and concerns that might not otherwise
be ventilated. On the other end of that prayer
line is a loving heavenly Father who has promised
to hear and answer our petitions.

DR. JAMES DOBSON

We shall come one day to a heaven where we shall gratefully know that God's great refusals were sometimes the true answers to our truest prayer.

P.T. FORSYTH

God is not interested in you praying perfectly; He just wants to spend time with you and be able to speak with you and know you are listening.

DR. HENRY CLOUD

Now I know in part, but then I will know fully just as I also have been fully known.

1 CORINTHIANS 13:12 NASB

Delight in the Lord

Delight yourself in the LORD
and he will give you the desires of your heart.
Commit your way to the LORD;
trust in him and he will do this:
He will make your righteousness shine
like the dawn,
the justice of your cause like the noonday sun.

PSALM 37:4–6 NIV

Open wide the windows of our spirits and fill
us full of light; open wide the door of our hearts,
that we may receive and entertain Thee with
all our powers of adoration.

CHRISTINA ROSSETTI

Send forth your light and your truth,
let them guide me;
let them bring me to your holy mountain,
to the place where you dwell.
Then will I go to the altar of God,
to God, my joy and my delight.

PSALM 43:3–4 NIV

Our fulfillment comes in knowing God's glory,
loving Him for it, and delighting in it.

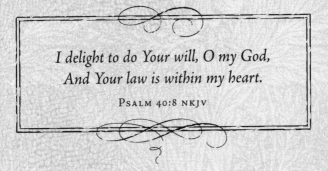

I delight to do Your will, O my God,
And Your law is within my heart.

PSALM 40:8 NKJV

Take Refuge

Let my soul take refuge...beneath the shadow
of Your wings: let my heart, this sea of restless
waves, find peace in You, O God.

AUGUSTINE

My Good Shepherd, who have shown Your very
gentle mercy to us,...give grace and strength to me,
Your little lamb, that in no tribulation or anguish
or pain may I turn away from You.

FRANCIS OF ASSISI

God stands fast as your rock, steadfast
as your safeguard, sleepless as your watcher,
valiant as your champion.

CHARLES H. SPURGEON

As for God, his way is perfect....
He is a shield for all who take refuge in him.

PSALM 18:30 NIV

I know that He who is far outside the whole
creation takes me within Himself and hides
me in His arms.... He is my heart,
He is in heaven: Both there and here He shows
Himself to me with equal glory.

SYMEON

Why would God promise a refuge unless He knew
we would need a place to hide once in a while?

NEVA COYLE

*The Lord is good,
a refuge in times of trouble.
He cares for those who trust in him.*

NAHUM 1:7 NIV

That I May Know Him

I want you woven into a tapestry of love,
in touch with everything there is to know of God.
Then you will have minds confident and at rest,
focused on Christ, God's great mystery. All the
richest treasures of wisdom and knowledge are
embedded in that mystery and nowhere else.

COLOSSIANS 2:2–3 MSG

He is a God who can be found. A God who
can be known. A God who wants to be close to us.
That's why He is called Immanuel,
which means "God with us." But He draws
close to us as we draw close to Him.

STORMIE OMARTIAN

Give us, Lord: a pure heart that we may
see Thee, a humble heart that we may
hear Thee, a heart of love that we may serve
Thee, a heart of faith that we may live with Thee.

DAG HAMMARSKJÖLD

Once the seeking heart finds God in personal
experience there will be no problem about loving
Him. To know Him is to love Him and to know
Him better is to love Him more.

A. W. TOZER

If anyone loves God, he is known by Him.

1 CORINTHIANS 8:3 NASB

The God of All Comfort

We may ask, "Why does God bring thunderclouds
and disasters when we want green pastures
and still waters?" Bit by bit, we find behind the
clouds, the Father's feet; behind the lightning,
an abiding day that has no night; behind the
thunder, a still small voice that comforts
with a comfort that is unspeakable.

OSWALD CHAMBERS

I look behind me and you're there,
then up ahead and you're there, too—
your reassuring presence, coming and going.
This is too much, too wonderful—
I can't take it all in!

PSALM 139:5–6 MSG

Regardless of the need, God comforts. He is the
God of all comfort! That's His specialty.

CHARLES R. SWINDOLL

God walks with us.... He scoops us up in His arms
or simply sits with us in silent strength until we
cannot avoid the awesome recognition that yes,
even now, He is here.

GLORIA GAITHER

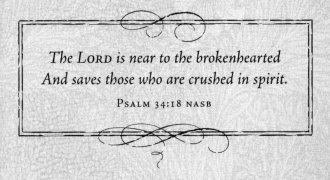

The LORD is near to the brokenhearted
And saves those who are crushed in spirit.

PSALM 34:18 NASB

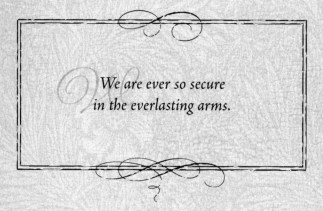

We are ever so secure
in the everlasting arms.